I Am Martin Luther King, Jr.

By Grace Norwich

Illustrated by
Elisabeth Alba

SCHOLASTIC INC.

ISBN 978-0-545-44780-5

10 9 8 7 6 5 4　　　　15 16 17/0

Printed in the U.S.A.　　40
First printing, December 2012

Cover illustration by Mark Fredrickson
Interior illustrations by Elisabeth Alba

Contents

Introduction

Change is hard. Most people don't like any kind of change. So you can imagine how hard it is to change strong beliefs. I'm talking about racism, and the idea that some folks are better than others just because of the color of their skin.

During my time, many Americans thought this was true. In some towns, black people couldn't stay in hotels or eat in restaurants. They even had separate water fountains for us, as if our dark skin was contagious! It didn't matter how well we did in school, how hard we worked at our jobs, or how devoted we were to our families, we were often thought of as ignorant, and even dangerous.

Despite their treatment, I always believed I was just as good as anyone else. So I set about changing not only people's hearts and minds, but also the laws of our land. As I put it in my famous "I Have a Dream" speech, my goal was that people of color, including my own children, could "one day live in a nation where they will not be judged by the color of their skin but by the content of their character."

It wasn't easy. Like I said, change is hard, even painful. Despite my brains, my supporters, and my skills as a speaker, I was challenged every day. But I never gave up believing and working toward my dream that "little black boys and black girls will be able to join hands with little white boys and white girls as sisters and brothers." I am Martin Luther King, Jr.

People You Will Meet

MARTIN LUTHER KING, JR.:
A great student who grew up to become a popular minister and one of the most important leaders of all time for his work to bring equality to all races using a nonviolent approach.

ALBERTA CHRISTINE WILLIAMS:
Martin's mother, a loving and educated woman, who attended college, which was unusual in her day. Her father was a minister at Ebenezer Baptist Church.

MARTIN LUTHER KING, SR.:
The son of sharecroppers, Martin, Sr., worked his way out of poverty, went to college, and became a minister at the Ebenezer Baptist Church in Atlanta.

CORETTA SCOTT:
Martin's wife, a college graduate and the mother of their four children, who continued to advocate for civil rights long after her husband's death.

ROSA PARKS:
A black seamstress who refused to follow the rules and move to the back of the bus, kicking off a massive bus boycott and the modern civil–rights movement.

JOHN F. KENNEDY:
The senator whose brother Robert helped get Martin out of jail, and who was elected the first Catholic president of the United States thanks in part to black voters. He was assassinated in 1963.

EUGENE "BULL" CONNOR:
Birmingham's public safety commissioner who threatened anyone who tried to bring white and black people together.

GEORGE WALLACE:
The Alabama governor who was so against integration that he broke the law to keep it from happening in his own state.

LYNDON B. JOHNSON:
The vice president who became president after John F. Kennedy's assassination, and who succeeded in getting the Civil Rights Act passed.

Time Line

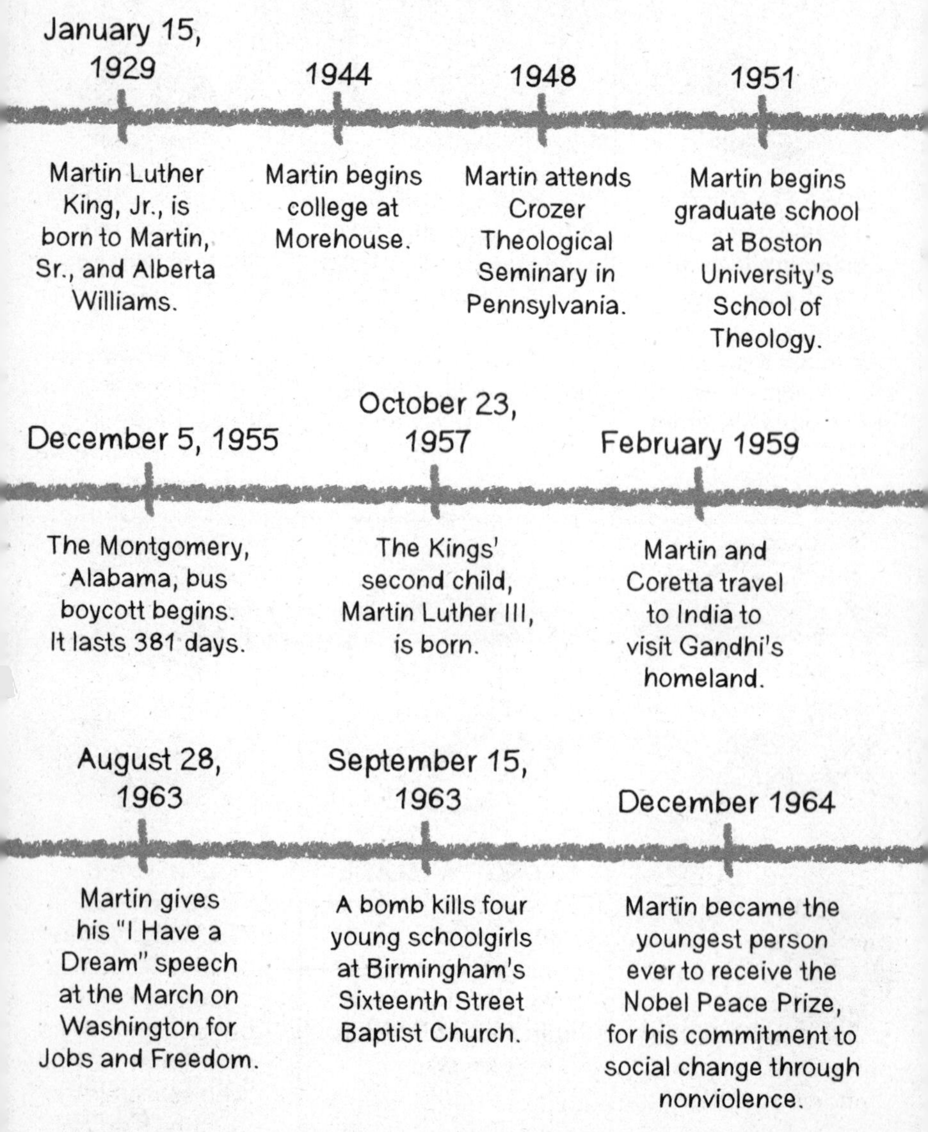

January 15, 1929
Martin Luther King, Jr., is born to Martin, Sr., and Alberta Williams.
1944
Martin begins college at Morehouse.
1948
Martin attends Crozer Theological Seminary in Pennsylvania.
1951
Martin begins graduate school at Boston University's School of Theology.
December 5, 1955
The Montgomery, Alabama, bus boycott begins. It lasts 381 days.
October 23, 1957
The Kings' second child, Martin Luther III, is born.
February 1959
Martin and Coretta travel to India to visit Gandhi's homeland.
August 28, 1963
Martin gives his "I Have a Dream" speech at the March on Washington for Jobs and Freedom.
September 15, 1963
A bomb kills four young schoolgirls at Birmingham's Sixteenth Street Baptist Church.
December 1964
Martin became the youngest person ever to receive the Nobel Peace Prize, for his commitment to social change through nonviolence.

June 18, 1953

Martin and Coretta Scott are married.

September 1, 1954

Martin becomes the pastor of Dexter Avenue Baptist Church in Montgomery, Alabama.

November 17, 1955

Martin and Coretta's first child, Yolanda Denise, is born.

January 30, 1961

The third King child, Dexter Scott, is born.

March 28, 1963

The fourth King child, Bernice Albertine, is born.

April 1963

Martin writes his famous Letter from Birmingham Jail.

March 25, 1965

Martin completes his march for equal voting rights from Selma to Montgomery with more than twenty thousand marchers.

April 4, 1968

Martin is assassinated on a motel balcony in Memphis, Tennessee.

1983

President Ronald Reagan signs a bill to create a federal holiday on the third Monday of January, near Martin's birthday, to celebrate the civil-rights hero.

An Early Lesson

The idea of right and wrong was part of Martin Luther King, Jr.'s, life from the moment he was born in Atlanta, Georgia, on January 15, 1929. That's because Martin's father *and* grandfather were both church ministers! And not just any ministers—they were both pastors of Ebenezer Baptist Church, which had the most influential African American **congregation** in Atlanta.

Martin, Sr., was a very large and strict man. He had high standards and a lot of rules, which he expected Martin, his older sister, Willie Christine, and his younger brother, Alfred Daniel, to obey.

If that seems harsh, perhaps it's because Martin, Sr., came from harsh circumstances. Born into a family of sharecroppers (farmers who worked on other people's land and were paid in just enough crops to survive), he grew up very poor. With his mother's support, he left home to go to Atlanta in search of a better life when he was only fifteen. Martin, Sr., worked extremely hard, earning his high-school degree and then attending Morehouse, a prestigious all-black college.

Martin's mother, Alberta, was quiet, loving, and very easy to talk to. But she was also smart, and accomplished something hardly any women, especially black women, did in those days—she earned a college degree. Alberta's father was a famous pastor at the

Visit Martin's Childhood Home and Church

In 1980, his house at 501 Auburn Avenue and other surrounding buildings—including the Ebenezer Baptist Church—became a National Historic Site. You can learn more about the site at www.thekingcenter.org.

Ebenezer Baptist Church, where her husband also became a minister. No wonder the church was a second home to Martin, Jr., who attended Sunday school and sang in the choir.

When he wasn't at church or at home, Martin was usually playing on his peaceful, shady block with a little white boy whose father had a store across the street from his house.

But when he turned six, Martin got his first bitter taste of the **prejudice** he'd spend the rest of his life fighting. The two best friends were sent to different schools. They were segregated, which means they were separated by color. The white boy went to one for white children, while Martin went to one for black children. That wasn't all. The white boy's father told him that he couldn't play with Martin anymore.

When Martin heard the news, he cried and cried. He didn't understand why they couldn't be friends. They both still liked to ride their bikes, fly model airplanes, and play ball. He had no clue about **racism**.

Martin's mom and dad had to sit him down to explain a fact that was hard for him to believe. Many white people didn't like black people because of the color

Segregation

During Martin's time, many places in the South enforced segregation with the Jim Crow laws. The laws were named for a white performer who was one of the first to use burnt cork to make his face look black, which was called blackface makeup. In the early 1800s, he made fun of black people by doing a silly song and dance as the character Jim Crow. The act was a big success and took him all over the country and even abroad. The name came to symbolize anything racist, including the laws that separated whites from blacks in schools, restaurants, movie theaters, and hotels. Under these regulations, black people had to ride in the back of the bus. And if they didn't, they could be thrown

in jail. In high school, Martin was returning home from a speech contest he'd won in a nearby town when the bus driver told him and his teacher they had to get up and give their seats to white people. Martin was angry, but it was the law of the land, so they rode the 90 miles home on their feet.

North/South Divide

In 1861, after Abraham Lincoln — who campaigned against expanding slavery beyond the states where it already existed — became president of the United States, eleven Southern states voted to secede. That meant they separated from the rest of the United States; they then formed their own country, which they called the Confederate States of America. This led to the Civil War, eventually won by the twenty-five other states, known as the Union, in 1865. The victory ended slavery in the entire nation, but racism lived on.

Abraham Lincoln

of their skin. He was dumbfounded and angry. How could anyone think like that?

His mother and father also explained that as Christians, it was important to forgive and not lash out at anyone, even racist whites who didn't think he was good enough to play with. It was a hard concept to wrap his head around, but one that would become the foundation for his beliefs. Martin's mom added one last idea: Even though they were asking him to forgive white people, he didn't need to believe what they thought about him. No matter what people said, he was just as good as anyone else and could make a difference in this world.

School Days

With the work ethic he learned from his father, the confidence he gained from his mother, and his own natural intelligence, it's not surprising that Martin was an excellent student. He pushed himself hard, which allowed him to skip two grades so that he graduated from Booker T. Washington High School when he was only fifteen years old.

As a teenager, Martin continued to experience segregation. In the summer after graduation, he got a glimpse of a world without it when he took a job working in tobacco fields in Connecticut. The North was by no means perfect, but it was inspiring for a southern black boy. There were no broken-down water fountains for black people or crumbling schools for black kids. And no sitting in the back of the bus! Coming back to Atlanta after the job

ended was hard. On the train home, he sat in any car like any other traveler who had paid his fare. By the time he changed trains in Washington, D.C., however, there were separate cars for black people. In the dining car, where he went to eat, he was forced to sit at a rear table with a curtain around him so that no white people could see him.

That type of humiliation never kept him from academic success. Following in his father's and grandfather's footsteps, Martin attended Morehouse, a **prestigious** all-black college in Atlanta.

While at college, Martin was already thinking about the next step: a career. He was torn between becoming a professor or a minister. Whatever he did, he knew he wanted to help people. Of course his grandfather and father were both ministers, but it turned out that one of his favorite professors at college was a minster, too. Plus, Martin had proved that he was very good at giving sermons, which is an important part of a pastor's job.

Morehouse was founded in 1867 to provide newly freed slaves with an education. The all-male school became the top college for many middle-class African Americans. Former Republican presidential candidate Herman Cain, filmmaker Spike Lee, actor Samuel L. Jackson, and Olympic gold medalist Edwin Moses are some of the school's famous alumni.

In 1948, when Martin received his diploma from Morehouse, his dad offered him a position in the family business—Ebenezer Baptist Church. But Martin had other plans. He wanted to keep studying. The following fall, he started school at Crozer Theological Seminary in Chester, Pennsylvania. At the seminary, which is a school where people study religion, there were only six black students out of a hundred. That was a stark contrast from Morehouse's all-black student body. But Martin didn't mind standing out.

Martin definitely *did* stand out at Crozer, but not because of his color. When he graduated in 1951, he was number one in his class. He also won a scholarship to get his **doctorate** at the graduate school of his choice. He chose Boston University School of Theology in Massachusetts, which turned out to be a great decision for more reasons than one.

Peaceful Influence

While at Crozer, Martin learned of Mahatma Gandhi, a thinker who would greatly influence the rest of his life. Born in 1869 in India, Gandhi studied to become a lawyer in London and then worked in South Africa, where blacks—and pretty much anyone of color, including Indians like himself—were treated

as inferior. He believed the best way to fight racism and discrimination of any kind was to protest peacefully through marches, fasts, and strikes. He called his nonviolent resistance method of making social change Soul Force. His kind of resistance was not about being passive but finding strength in practicing nonviolent methods. When he returned to India, he brought his theory of nonviolence with him and earned the title Mahatma, or "Great Soul." He used the same methods to help his country gain its independence from England in 1947.

DSONS
N'S
GILCHRIS

Martin Falls in Love

It didn't take long for Martin to make new friends in Boston, and the most important one he made was Coretta Scott. Originally from Alabama, where her father was a farmer, the pretty young woman was musical and smart. She had graduated from college with a degree in music and elementary education. Like Martin, she had won a grant to continue her studies, which she was doing at the New England Conservatory of Music in Boston. The pair went on a date in their new city, and they talked about everything that was important to them—family, racism, peace. Coretta was beautiful, intelligent, and clearly a good person. That was enough for Martin. After one hour in Coretta's presence, he knew she was the one for him.

There was only one issue that needed to be resolved. Coretta dreamed about becoming a concert singer, but Martin wanted a wife who would stay home and raise a family while he went out and shook up the world. In the end, Martin won (he was a very persuasive man) and the two were married on June 18, 1953. The ceremony, officiated by Martin's father, was held on the lawn of Coretta's family's home in Marion, Alabama.

If Coretta was going to be a homemaker, that meant Martin had to find a job. In 1954, Martin traveled to the Dexter Avenue Baptist

Church in Montgomery, Alabama, to be a guest preacher. During the four-hour drive to Montgomery, he was filled with mixed emotions. He knew that the church would offer him the position of pastor if he didn't blow the speech. Martin liked that it was a prestigious congregation filled with educated members, including doctors, lawyers, and professors. Still, he was uneasy about starting a life with his new wife in the South. If they remained in the North, they would live in a world where blacks were treated more fairly.

During his lifetime, Martin became famous for his amazing sermons. His ability to communicate through the spoken word wasn't just a gift from God. He worked really hard at it! On average, Martin spent fifteen hours writing each sermon and learning it by heart.

Sure enough, Martin awed the congregants with his ability to talk with passion and intelligence. He would regularly speak without using any notes. The job was his if he wanted it. He and Coretta debated the pros and cons, and in the end he started the job on September 1, 1954, at the age of twenty-five. They might be less comfortable in Montgomery, a city smack-dab in the segregated South, but they would have a real opportunity to make a difference.

Sore Feet and High Spirits

Martin had been in Montgomery for just over a year when an ordinary lady did something extraordinary.

On December 1, 1955, a seamstress named Rosa Parks, tired of always moving to the back of the bus during the rides she took to and from her job at a local department store, decided she was going to sit up front. The small forty-two-year-old seamstress ignored the bus driver's orders to move to the back of the bus, and was

arrested by the police. Her refusal kicked off the **civil-rights** movement in America.

For Martin, his first year in Montgomery had been a busy one. Not only had he and Coretta welcomed their first child, Yolanda Denise, in November, but he was also working hard at his job. As pastor of Dexter Avenue Baptist Church, he spent a lot of time trying to convince his congregants to stand up for their rights. He encouraged them to register to vote so they could change racist laws, as well as join the National Association for the Advancement of Colored People.

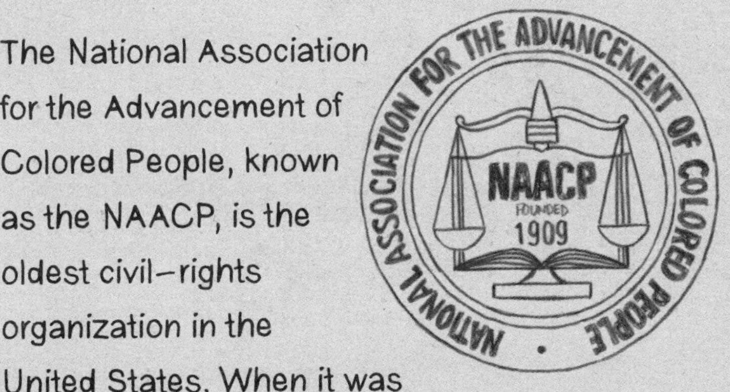

The National Association for the Advancement of Colored People, known as the NAACP, is the oldest civil-rights organization in the United States. When it was started on February 12, 1909, it was mostly made up of white people (although Martin's maternal grandfather, A. D. Williams, was one of the founding members). The NAACP fought against Jim Crow laws and lynching, which was a common practice in which a group of people practiced violence against blacks, often by way of hanging.

Martin and other local black leaders wanted to support Rosa. It wasn't right for a woman to be thrown in jail for just trying to sit down on the bus. He remembered his own humiliating experience when he had to get up for white people on the bus as a high-school student. "It was the angriest I have ever been in my life," he said.

They decided to protest the poor treatment of Rosa and all blacks by holding a boycott of the city buses. A boycott is a peaceful protest, in the tradition of Gandhi, in which a large group of people refuses to buy goods or participate in services until a policy change is made. In this case, the blacks of Montgomery weren't going to ride the buses (and the bus company would

7582

lose a lot of money in fares) until the rule about moving to the back changed.

Boycotts don't work unless nearly everybody participates. So in Montgomery, they printed and handed out thousands of flyers about the bus boycott, and the day before its official start, the leaders preached about it during their Sunday sermons. Still, the next day, Monday, December 5, no one was sure if it would work. Maybe not enough black people would join the protest for anyone in the bus company to care.

That morning, Coretta looked out the window of her home and saw a bus ride by—without a single person inside! She called to her husband to come look. He did, and soon he saw the same thing. Over and over, buses kept rolling by completely empty! The black community had embraced the boycott wholeheartedly. People walked to school, jobs, and anywhere else, going as far as ten miles by foot.

As the boycott wore on, Martin organized a huge car pool so that blacks wouldn't have to spend all their money on taxis or walk for hours (he even raised money to buy a bunch of station wagons for the effort). Even though city leaders worried the bus company was going bankrupt, they refused to back down. As the main leader behind the protest, Martin received threatening phone calls to his house and was jailed for driving 30 miles per hour in a 25-mile-per-hour zone. The most vicious attack, however, came in the form of a firebomb that hit the porch of his house. It destroyed the porch and the front windows, but luckily didn't harm Coretta or Yolanda.

The black community was understandably enraged. They wanted to get revenge, but Martin, who should have been the angriest, told them not to resort to violence. "We must meet hate with love," he said. The best thing they could do was not give up, he argued, and the black people of Montgomery did just that . . . for 381 days!

The boycott ended over a year later, on December 20, 1956, when the Supreme Court ruled that black people could sit wherever they wanted. The highest court in the land declared

Martin's first book was *Stride Toward Freedom: The Montgomery Story*.

segregated buses **unconstitutional**. Martin celebrated the huge victory for blacks all over the country by taking a bus ride on December 21 and sitting right up front.

A National Pulpit

The new bus laws were a huge step, but they were just the beginning. Martin wanted to take his message of equality to the entire nation.

On May 17, 1957, he and twenty thousand other black and white citizens did just that when they gathered at the Lincoln Memorial for the Prayer Pilgrimage in Washington, D.C. The purpose of the massive event was to demand the passage of a civil-rights bill. Martin made a speech that asked President Dwight D.

Dwight D. Eisenhower

Eisenhower to ensure equal rights under the law—including the right to vote—for all people in the United States. While women and blacks had the right to vote, there were still a lot of obstacles put in their way. In many places in the South, black voters were turned away for all kinds of reasons. They were asked to pay poll taxes or take difficult reading and writing tests. Even though that kind of thing was against the law, it happened all the time.

The success of the Montgomery bus boycott had made Martin famous (reporters and photographers covered him smiling at the front of the bus). The Prayer Pilgrimage, however, was the first time that many people all over the country had a chance to hear him speak. His rousing, heartfelt words electrified the nation and in an instant turned him into the country's unofficial head of the black community. After the event in D.C., Vice President Richard Nixon met with Martin. It was the first time anyone in the Eisenhower White House reached out to a black leader.

This massive responsibility took a toll on his life as a father and a husband. Because he couldn't be around that much, Coretta was left to manage their family, which continued to grow with the birth of Martin Luther King III on October 23, 1957.

Although Coretta had her hands full taking care of two small children while Martin tried to change the world, she accompanied him on a very special trip to India in 1959. They spent a month making their own **pilgrimage**

to places important to Martin's hero, Gandhi. They went to his birthplace in Porbandar and to the Amniabad ashram where Gandhi started his 218-mile walk to a place called Bambi. Starting with eight people, the Indian leader gradually walked with millions in protest of a tax on salt.

Martin returned home inspired to make peaceful protest an instrument of good in his part of the world. "I left India more convinced than ever before that nonviolent resistance is the most potent weapon available to oppressed people in their struggle for freedom," he wrote.

To reach a much bigger audience than the one he found in front of him on Sundays, he had to leave the Dexter Avenue Baptist Church. Of course, the congregation was upset. Anyone giving sermons was bound to be a major letdown after Martin. But they also understood. "History has thrust upon me a responsibility from which I cannot turn away," he said in his good-bye sermon.

The same year of his trip to India, the King family moved to Atlanta so Martin could focus his efforts on civil rights. Not that he gave up being a minister. He made his father's wish come true by becoming co-pastor of his family's Ebenezer Baptist Church.

Atlanta might have been his home base, but Martin was now truly a national figure. Because of his high profile, he could mobilize a lot of people. However, it also made him a target for racists, including law officials who wanted to make an example out of him.

In addition to marches, those who were part of the civil-rights movement participated in sit-ins, in which black and white students would go to whites-only lunch counters in the South and sit, waiting to be served, until the police pulled them out.

When Martin participated in a sit-in at a department-store lunch counter in Atlanta on October 19, 1960, it was almost certain that he'd

be arrested. Sure enough he was taken to the Fulton County jail, which became filled with two hundred students arrested for protesting that day.

For simply sitting at a lunch counter, Martin was sentenced to four months of hard labor in the state penitentiary! The excuse for such a harsh punishment was that this was his second offense (he had been arrested months earlier for a traffic violation). Coretta, pregnant with their third child, Dexter, who was born the following January, fell down sobbing when she heard the verdict.

Despite his fame, stature, and important friends, Martin was stuck in jail. His supporters tried everything to get him out. For help, they approached Vice President Richard Nixon and Senator John F. Kennedy, both of whom were running for president. And both ignored their pleas, afraid that they'd upset white voters by taking action. Urged by his friends, Senator Kennedy did call Coretta to comfort her. More important, though, his brother Robert called the judge who had sent Martin to jail and freed the civil-rights leader.

John F. Kennedy

That November, Senator Kennedy broke through his own barrier of prejudice by becoming the first Catholic president (something a lot of people had said would never happen). By all accounts, he never would have won without the help of black voters, who appreciated what his family had done for Martin.

TANDY DINER
WHITE'S ONLY
TANDY DINER

CHAPTER SIX

Bombingham

The Supreme Court, the highest court in America, had proclaimed segregation illegal, but in everyday life, blacks still didn't have the same rights as whites. Throughout the South, they were barred from restaurants and bathrooms, universities and lunch counters. President Kennedy sent a civil-rights bill to Congress but was not doing much to get it passed.

A federal law was only way to ensure that

...n Americans would have their rights enforced no matter where they were in the country, but it seemed like a lot of white people wouldn't change their ways no matter what.

Instead of being discouraged by the situation, Martin took it as a challenge to go to the heart of segregation—Birmingham, Alabama—and try to change things there. It might have been against the law in the rest of the country, but in that town segregation *was* the law. Eugene "Bull" Connor, who as the public safety commissioner ran the police force, threatened anyone who tried to bring white and black people together.

Eugene "Bull" Connor

Martin and other black leaders took the place by storm—peacefully, that is.

Project C

Known as the most segregated city in the country, Birmingham had an active chapter of the Ku Klux Klan. The white–supremacist group, whose members are known for wearing white robes and tall white hats that cover their faces, beat up, shot, and lynched black people. Klansmen, as they were called, bombed so many African American homes and institutions in Birmingham that the city got the nickname Bombingham.

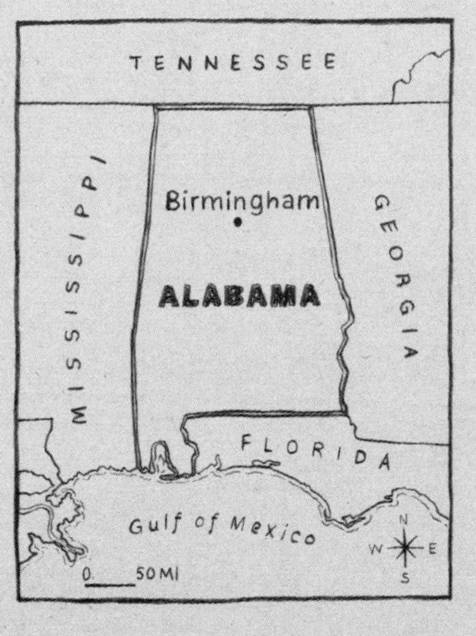

Maybe that's why Martin and the other black leaders had to give their protests there a code name, Project C (the C stood for *confrontation*).

In the spring of 1963, they gathered members of Birmingham's black community, who were very frightened of Bull. In meetings and services, they inspired them through songs and stories to take action. Not surprisingly, the Birmingham establishment did not take kindly to the sit-ins staged at local lunch counters. Within the first three days, thirty-five protesters had been arrested. After a week, 102 were in jail.

The leaders of the protest met in Martin's Birmingham motel room on April 12 to figure out what to do next. It was Good Friday, and Martin's dad was there because he wanted Martin to come home to preach Easter Sunday. Some of the other leaders wanted him to stay in Birmingham to personally lead a protest. A third group wanted him to stay off the streets and instead work to get people out of jail.

Martin had a decision to make, and it wasn't easy. A lot of people were counting on him to

do the right thing. He left the men and went into his bedroom to pray. When he returned, everyone knew his decision without him having to say a word. Normally, Martin wore nice suits, but he was wearing jeans. He only wore those when he was going to jail. He had decided to protest.

Martin led fifty people in a march toward

city hall; everybody was arrested within minutes. Once in jail, Martin was denied all his rights. Sitting in solitary confinement, he wasn't allowed to make even one phone call. He knew Coretta, who had just given birth to their fourth child, Bernice, would be worried sick if she didn't hear from him.

Easter Sunday came and still he wasn't allowed to contact anyone on the outside. His mind was racing with thoughts. Locked up in a dark cell while the world outside was in turmoil, it would have been easy for Martin to doubt himself. But he was a man of unshakable faith in his mission. Even when a group of eight white ministers published a letter in the *Birmingham News*

stating the protests in Birmingham were wrong because they created more violence, Martin didn't waver. The white pastors admitted there were social injustices, but they believed the problems should be fought in court and not on the street.

Martin needed to respond, but how? He didn't have any paper to write a letter. He had faced bigger obstacles before. Over the rest of his eight days in jail, with only toilet paper and the edges of newspaper available, Martin passionately argued, in a letter that would make history, that unjust laws should not be obeyed.

Martin spent the week in jail with many of the other black adults in Birmingham. In order to keep the protests going, one of the main organizers came up with the idea of having children march. Martin, worried about the kids' safety, didn't approve. But on May 2, over a thousand children, from six-year-olds

Letter from Birmingham Jail

Martin smuggled out his 6,500-word essay on scraps of paper handed to his lawyers, who brought them back to the leaders' headquarters. In his letter, he addressed the white clergymen's concerns, including the idea that this was not a good time for the protests. "Justice too long delayed is justice denied," he said, quoting the former British prime minister William Ewart Gladstone. Martin's Letter from Birmingham Jail, as the piece became known, was reprinted many times in magazines and books.

to teenagers, sang during a four-hour march. Bull Connor didn't care how old they were. He arrested them, too! More than nine hundred kids were crowded into police vans and school buses and carted off to jail.

That wasn't even the worst of it. Later that day, Bull ordered the use of fire hoses and police dogs on any kids marching or people watching. The horrifying images of children being slammed against walls by pounding water while dogs attacked were reported and photographed by journalists, who brought the story to homes throughout America. People across the country, angry and upset over what they saw, began to support the civil-rights movement.

At the same time, the white residents of Birmingham were sick

Freedom Riders

On May 4, 1961, two buses filled with students started off from Washington, D.C., to stage peaceful protests throughout the South. But they were cut short in Alabama, where locals shot out the tires of one bus and threw a bomb in the other. The students obviously couldn't go any farther. That was the end of the trip, but not the movement. Soon more students, who became known as

Freedom Riders, took buses south to protest segregation. When the Freedom Riders and Martin met in Montgomery, Alabama, a crowd outside threw bottles and stones at the First Baptist Church of Atlanta. A brick hit a stained–glass window, shattering it and sending glass over some of the people inside. They were scared, but Martin told them, "Fear not, we've come too far to turn back."

of the violence, and the business owners were sick of losing money. They negotiated with the marchers and agreed not only to desegregate the city but also to create a group made up of black and white people for better race relations.

Birmingham proved the power of nonviolent protest, which swept the nation. Black people all over stood up—or sat down—for their rights.

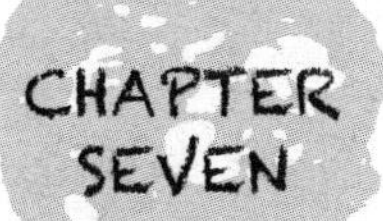

The Dream

Some people still refused to accept that the world was changing and that segregation was a thing of the past.

Alabama governor George Wallace was one of those people. He hated **integration** so much that he broke the law to keep it from happening. On June 11, 1963, he defied a federal court order allowing two black students to attend the University of Alabama, which was the last segregated state university in the country.

He actually stood in front of the school's administration building to bar the students' entry with his own body. That's how much he didn't want them to come in! President Kennedy ordered the Alabama National Guard to remove the governor and let in the students.

There was no doubt about it. Black Americans needed a federal law that would

George Wallace had a long career in public life. He ran for governor for the fourth time in 1982. During that race, though, he was a very different candidate. He apologized for being against integration earlier in his life and wound up winning the majority of black votes and winning the position.

George Wallace

ensure their rights no matter if they lived in Alabama or Alaska.

The night after the incident with George Wallace, President Kennedy told the country he would send a civil-rights bill to Congress that would give all Americans the same access to public places. To support the president in this effort, Martin and other black leaders led a march to Washington, D.C., that was one of the biggest the country had ever seen.

On August 28, Martin was amazed at the sea of people stretched out across the Washington Mall. The turnout for the March on Washington for Jobs and Freedom exceeded his expectations. He couldn't possibly have imagined that more than two hundred fifty thousand Americans from all over the country

"I Have a Dream"

Out of a number of leaders who addressed the crowd, Martin was the last to speak. It didn't matter that there were a quarter of a million people waiting and listening. Like always, Martin didn't use notes. His speech, which was only supposed to be four minutes, had a very formal tone. But after Mahalia Jackson, a famous singer who was on the podium with him, said, "Tell them about your dream, Martin. Tell them about the dream," he began improvising and changing the original speech he planned to give.

"I have a dream that one day this nation will rise up and live out the true meaning of its creed: 'We hold these truths to be self-evident: that all men are created equal,'" he said. "I have a dream that one day on the

red hills of Georgia, sons of former slaves and the sons of former slave owners will be able to sit down together at the table of brotherhood."

The crowd came alive when Martin talked about his dream of a world where race no longer mattered. They encouraged him to go on, and he did for more than sixteen minutes!

"I have a dream that my four little children will one day live in a nation where they will not be judged by the color of their skin but by the content of their character," he said.

would travel to D.C. that day to show their support for a civil-rights bill. No wonder the rally became known as the Great March on Washington. Thirty special trains and twenty thousand chartered buses were needed to bring the people to D.C. Meanwhile, not all of them arrived by bus or by train. An eighty-two-year-old bicycled all the way from Ohio, while another man biked from South Dakota. One man roller-skated from Chicago, which took him eleven days!

Famous Faces at the Great March

Sidney Poitier

Charlton Heston

Lena Horne

Sammy Davis, Jr.

Marlon Brando

Racial unity, however, was still just a dream. On September 15, 1963, less than three weeks after the Great March, the Ku Klux Klan set off a bomb in Birmingham's Sixteenth Street Baptist Church. Denise McNair, Carole Robertson, Cynthia Wesley, and Addie Mae Collins, four girls attending Bible class, were killed. None of them was older than fourteen.

Martin, mourning the senseless loss of innocent lives, went straight to the city he had worked so hard to change to make sure no black people tried to seek vengeance. He wanted to stop those who wanted to hurt black people, but not through violence. "We must be concerned not merely about who murdered them, but about the system, the way of life, and the philosophy which produced the murderers," he said at the eulogy he delivered for three of the four girls.

The sixties were a challenging time. The civil-rights movement was one of only a number of revolutions happening in society. People all over were actively trying to change the world. Sometimes, however, the wrong people took matters into their own hands. The nation was stunned when President Kennedy was shot in Dallas, Texas, on November 22, 1963.

Only five days later, while Americans were still mourning the loss of a beloved president, Lyndon B. Johnson, who had become president, asked Congress to pass the civil-rights bill in honor of President Kennedy. "No memorial oration or eulogy could more eloquently honor President Kennedy's memory than the earliest possible passage of the civil-rights bill for which he fought so long," he said. President Johnson's plea worked, and on July 2, 1964, he signed the Civil Rights Act with Martin right by his side.

Nobel Peace Prize

In 1964, Martin received one of the world's most prestigious honors, the Nobel Peace Prize, for proving that change can happen without force. He was only thirty-five years old, making him not only the third black person but also the youngest person in history to ever receive the prize.

The Nobel Peace Prize was created by the Swedish chemist Alfred B. Nobel. Rich from inventing dynamite, he left $9 million after he died in 1896 to be given out annually to people who have done amazing things in the following five subjects: peace, literature, physics, chemistry, and physiology or medicine. A sixth subject, **economics**, became an awards category in 1968.

Civil Rights Act of 1964

The federal bill put an end to the Jim Crow laws. Discrimination in any public place, like a park, a community swimming pool, or a library, was officially against the law in all states (discrimination was also forbidden in places the public visited, like movie theaters, hotels, or restaurants). A new law also went into effect stating that companies with more than fifteen employees could no longer discriminate among their workers.

Although it followed the death of a great leader, the passage of the Civil Rights Act was a cause for celebration. That had been one of the civil-rights movement's major goals.

President Johnson signed seventy-two copies of the Civil Rights Act to give as souvenirs to the people attending the historic moment.

BALLOT BOX
STUB BOX

The Right to Vote

The one important area the Civil Rights Act did not protect was voting rights. Nowhere was the right of black people to vote more trampled on than in Selma, Alabama. Although half the residents in the county were black, only one percent of the voting-age black community was registered to vote. That's because there were a number of stumbling blocks in the way of getting people signed up. The literacy test to qualify to vote was as hard as a college exam, and the office to register was only open a few days each month during a time when most people were at work. This was no accident, but a direct effort to keep black people out of the polls.

Setting his sights on righting this wrong, Martin organized marches to Selma's courthouse to vote, but it was illegal to march in the city, so thousands of black people, including Martin, went to jail. Those who opposed civil rights were prepared for a fight using every weapon they had. During a voter-registration drive, a twenty-six-year-old protestor named Jimmie Lee Jackson was shot and killed by a state trooper.

In the face of the violence Alabama's law enforcement was willing to use, Martin planned a 54-mile march from Selma to Montgomery, which Governor George Wallace immediately banned. Despite the ban, over six hundred

marchers started walking on Sunday, March 7, 1965, until they came upon a wall of state troopers, who attacked them. Seventy people were hurt in the assault that included clubs, tear gas, and horses.

The images of attacks on innocent people that day, which became known as Bloody Sunday, shocked and angered the nation—

including Martin, who hadn't been with the protestors because he'd been in Atlanta preaching.

Upset that he hadn't been by the side of the protestors, he organized another march for March 9. When he left on that march with fifteen hundred people, the same thing happened: They faced fierce state troopers ready to beat them down. Martin put a stop to the march. He wanted to help blacks, not kill them.

After hearing what had happened, President Johnson assured Martin that the next time they tried to do their 54-mile march, he would send troops to protect them. What followed was like a dream come true to Martin. On March 21, four thousand people from all races and religions, regions of the country, professions, and ages came together to protest in peace. Four days later, during the final six miles to Montgomery, twenty-five thousand people marched together to hand a **petition** demanding voting rights for black people to Governor Wallace in Montgomery's capitol building.

The law was now fully on the side of all people—black, white, or any color. But just because black people now had the right to vote or to eat in any restaurant they wanted

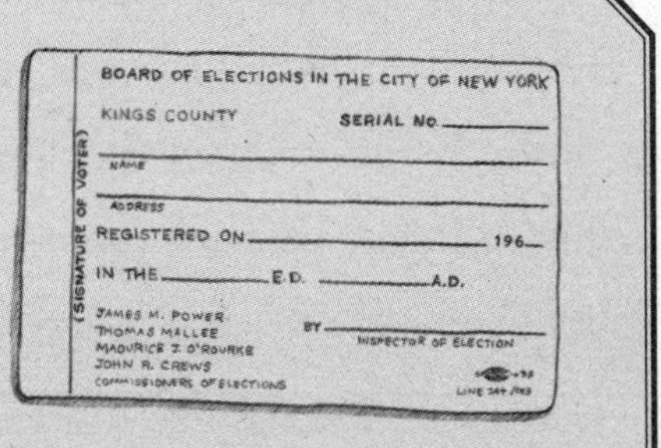

BOARD OF ELECTIONS IN THE CITY OF NEW YORK
KINGS COUNTY SERIAL No. ____
(SIGNATURE OF VOTER)
NAME
ADDRESS
REGISTERED ON ____ 196_
IN THE ____ E.D. ____ A.D.
JAMES M. POWER
THOMAS MALLEE
MAURICE J. O'ROURKE
JOHN R. CREWS
COMMISSIONERS OF ELECTIONS
BY ____
INSPECTOR OF ELECTION

On August 6, 1965, President Johnson signed the Voting Rights Act that gave every citizen an equal right to vote, which meant no more literacy tests or other obstacles. Rosa Parks and Martin were right by the president's side while he signed it.

didn't change the fact that they had suffered hundreds of years under racism. Without the same access to education and jobs, they didn't have an equal shot at living a good life.

Some black people started to question what the civil-rights movement had really given them. The laws might have changed but so many opportunities were still closed to them. Many poor blacks were fed up, and Martin started to lose some of his followers to frustration.

This anger came to a violent boil in the Los Angeles neighborhood of Watts during the hot summer month of August 1965. It started when a black man named Marquette Frye was pulled over by the cops for driving dangerously. A group gathered around the police as they arrested Marquette and his brother, Ronald. They shouted at the officers, accusing them of being racists and saying that the only violation the men had committed was to have the wrong

skin color. The crowd grew bigger and angrier until they started attacking the police.

The police sent at least twenty cars to block off the neighborhood of Watts so no one could get in or out. When news of the blockade spread through the area, people were angry about being caged in by the police like animals. They joined the crowd until the situation turned into a full-blown riot. People took out all their rage on the place they lived, breaking windows, setting fires, looting merchandise from inside stores, and totaling cars. The riot didn't end until six days later, when the U.S. Army stormed the neighborhood and put a stop to it.

Watts Riot by the Numbers

6 days of rioting

34 people killed

1,000 injured

600 buildings looted

$50–$100 million estimated in total damage

FRAGILE

Civil-Rights Struggle Marches On

In 1966, the Kings moved to Chicago, which was known as the Birmingham of the North. White people in the city wouldn't allow blacks to hold good jobs or let them rent decent homes. Even worse, black people often were charged more for places to live.

A perfect example was the King family's apartment, which was run-down and cost $90 a month. That might not sound like a lot today,

but if they had been white they could have rented a bigger and better apartment in the white neighborhood for $10 less a month!

Martin was a world leader and could have lived in a nicer place, but he wanted his kids to understand how most black people lived. It turned out they weren't the only ones who got a lesson on what it meant to be poor. Not too long after the move, the King kids started acting out, which was unusual for them. Martin realized it was because they had nowhere to play. Poor neighborhoods lacked the playgrounds, lawns, and parks of richer ones.

Never had he been more convinced of the need to protest on behalf of economic fairness. In late 1967, Martin announced the next evolution of the civil-rights struggle. Called the Poor People's Campaign, it used the same nonviolent action to put an end to poverty not only for blacks but also for Latinos, whites, and anyone else struggling economically. Martin had big plans for the campaign: Instead of a one-day march, people would camp out on the Mall in Washington, D.C., starting in April 1968, and stay until the government agreed to the demand for a $30 billion antipoverty program.

It was a bold plan, but if anyone could pull it off it was Martin. On April 4, 1968, Martin was in Memphis, Tennessee, helping striking garbage workers, who were mainly black, get a raise. He had a lot of work to do to make the campout on the Mall happen, but the sanitation strike was a perfect example of how race and economics went hand in hand, so he wanted to be there.

Unfortunately, Martin never got a chance to see his Poor People's Campaign through. That night, while he stood on the balcony of his room at the Lorraine Motel in Memphis, before leaving for dinner, a gunshot rang out. A bullet came out of nowhere and hit him in the neck. Martin Luther King, Jr., was killed at the age of thirty-nine.

"I may not get there with you," Martin had said in a sermon the night before he was murdered.

Martin's Killer

While he was trying to get into England, James Earl Ray was arrested in London on June 8, 1968, for Martin's murder. The serial criminal, whose robberies had landed him in prison three times, confessed to the murder (later he tried to take it back) and was sentenced to ninety-nine years in prison, where he died in 1998 at the age of seventy.

James Earl Ray

Representatives John Conyers of Michigan and Shirley Chisholm of New York introduced a bill to create a federal holiday in Martin's honor every session of Congress for fifteen years until they succeeded in getting it passed and President Ronald Reagan signed it into law.

Ronald Reagan

"But I want you to know tonight, that we, as a people, will get to the Promised Land."

The days after Martin's death said a lot about the life he led. A few days after he was killed, President Johnson signed a bill known as the Fair Housing Act, which made any kind of discrimination when it comes to housing illegal. Also in the days after his funeral, Coretta, despite her grief, held a march for the

Memphis sanitation workers, who eventually got the pay increase they were looking for.

Coretta never stopped working to carry out her husband's legacy. She fought to improve civil rights until her death in 2006. Someone had cut her husband's life short, but nobody could stop his dream. Happily, Coretta lived to see a federal holiday instituted in honor of her husband in 1986.

Martin Luther King, Jr., altered the destiny not only of a race, but also of an entire country. He made America, and the world, a better place to live. He won awards and international fame for his commitment to his ideals of the equality of all humans and of nonviolence as the only valid method for change. He could mobilize thousands to protest, and he commanded the attention of presidents. He was also a moving preacher, husband, and father. All of these elements are part of his legacy. But how did Martin want to be remembered? What was important to him? In a sermon he delivered two months before his death, he talked about what he wanted mourners to think about at his funeral. He didn't want people to go on about his awards or how great he was at giving speeches. Instead, he said, "I'd like somebody to mention that day, that Martin Luther King, Jr., tried to give his life serving others."

Famous Quotes

"Faith is taking the first step, even when you don't see the whole staircase."

•

"Injustice anywhere is a threat to justice everywhere."

•

"If a man is called to be a street sweeper, he should sweep streets even as Michelangelo painted, or Beethoven composed music, or Shakespeare wrote poetry. He should sweep streets so well that all the hosts of heaven and earth will pause to say, here lived a great street sweeper who did his job well."

•

"Let no man pull you low enough to hate him."

"Our lives begin to end the day we become silent about things that matter."

•

"The ultimate measure of a man is not where he stands in moments of comfort and convenience, but where he stands at times of challenge and controversy."

•

"I submit to you that if a man hasn't discovered something he will die for, he isn't fit to live."

•

"In the end, we will remember not the words of our enemies, but the silence of our friends."

You Should Know About Martin Luther King, Jr.

1. Martin Luther King, Jr., was born on January 15, 1929, to Martin, Sr., and Alberta Williams. The middle of three children, he grew up in Atlanta, Georgia.

2. After graduating high school when he was only fifteen years old, Martin attended Morehouse College and then Crozer Theological Seminary, where he graduated first in his class and earned a scholarship to graduate school in Boston.

U.S. postage stamp

Martin knew he wanted to marry Coretta Scott after knowing her for just one hour.

Martin's first real job was as the minister of the Dexter Avenue Baptist Church in Montgomery, Alabama.

A firebomb hit and destroyed the porch of Martin and Coretta's house in Montgomery during the bus boycott, but he never resorted to anger or violence.

One of Martin's biggest heroes was the Indian leader Mahatma Gandhi because of his teachings on nonviolence.

7

Martin was sent to jail many times for participating in all kinds of protests.

8

Martin played a huge role in getting the Civil Rights Act of 1964 (which made discrimination in public places illegal) signed into law.

After the Civil Rights Act was passed, Martin set his sights on gaining economic and political justice for poor people.

Martin's death ushered in the passage of the Fair Housing Act, which made discrimination in the sale or renting of homes illegal.

Statue in Washington, D.C.

That Are Pretty Cool to Know

MLK was named after his father—Michael. When he was born, his name was Michael Luther King, Jr. But when he turned five, his father changed both their names to Martin.

Martin and Coretta had to spend their wedding night in the guest quarters of a funeral home because, at the time they got married, hotels in Alabama wouldn't give rooms to black people.

Martin never stopped learning. During his first year as a minister, he read at least twenty-six books and 102 magazines.

The first person who tried to take Martin's life was a black person! In 1858, during a book signing of *Stride Toward Freedom* in Harlem, a woman stabbed him with a letter opener. Surgeons had to perform a complicated procedure to take out the weapon, which was next to his heart's main artery. If his attacker, later committed to an insane asylum, had come less than an inch closer, she would have killed him.

5 The "I Have a Dream" speech, which he used to end the March on Washington, was similar to one he had delivered many times—in fact, he had delivered it to insurance executives in Detroit only a week before.

6 After President Kennedy was assassinated, Martin predicted his own death, telling Coretta, "I don't think I'm going to live to reach forty."

7 Martin was the first African American named *Time* magazine's Man of the Year, in 1963. It was a huge honor, but the article said he didn't have a sense of humor, which Martin did not find funny.

Time cover

Martin took the $54,000 from the Nobel Peace Prize and gave it to civil-rights groups.

The words on Martin's tombstone, taken from a spiritual, are "Free at last, Free at last, / Thank God Almighty / I'm Free at last."

Martin Luther King, Jr., Day is celebrated on the third Monday in January so that it can be close to his birthday, on January 15.

Glossary

Civil rights: the individual rights that all members of a society have to freedom and equal treatment under the law

Congregation: a group of people assembled for religious worship

Doctorate: the highest academic degree given by a college or university

Economics: the study of the way that money, resources, and services are used in a society

Integration: the act or practice of making facilities or an organization open to people of all races

Petition: a letter signed by many people asking those in power to change their policy or actions

Pilgrimage: a long journey

Prejudice: an unfair opinion about someone based on the person's race, religion, or other characteristic

Prestigious: greatly respected or of high status, due to being successful, powerful, rich, or famous

Racism: the belief that a particular race is better than others or treating people unfairly because of their race

Unconstitutional: not in keeping with the basic principles or laws set forth in the Constitution of the United States

Places to Visit

Visit some of the historic places from Martin Luther King, Jr.'s life.

Martin's Birthplace

nps.gov/malu/planyourvisit/birth_home_tours.htm

Ebenezer Baptist Church

nps.gov/malu/planyourvisit/ebenezer_baptist_church.htm

The National Civil Rights Museum at the Lorraine Motel

civilrightsmuseum.org

The King Center

thekingcenter.org

Martin Luther King, Jr. National Memorial

mlkmemorial.org

Bibliography

The Civil Rights Movement for Kids: A History with 21 Activities, Mary C. Turck, Chicago Review Press, 2000.

Don't Know Much About Martin Luther King Jr., Kenneth C. Davis, Amistad, 2006.

Martin Luther King, Jr.: A Dream of Hope, Alice Fleming, Sterling Publishing Company, 2008.

Martin Luther King, Jr. and the March on Washington, Frances E. Ruffin, Grosset & Dunlap, 2001.

The Martin Luther King, Jr., Encyclopedia, Clayborne Carson, Tenisha Armstrong, Susan Carson, Erin Cook, and Susan Englander, Greenwood Press, 2008.

10 Days: Martin Luther King Jr., David Colbert, Aladdin Paperbacks, 2008.

Who Was Martin Luther King, Jr.?, Bonnie Bader, Grosset & Dunlap, 2008.

The Words of Martin Luther King, Jr., selected by Coretta Scott King, Newmarket Press, 1983.

Index

Also Available: